T0128914

Enlighten Up

*A Medium's Perspective on Becoming
the Light That's Inside of You*

ANGELA BLANCHET

BALBOA.
PRESS

A DIVISION OF HAY HOUSE

Balboa Press books may be ordered through booksellers or by contacting:

Balboa Press
A Division of Hay House
1663 Liberty Drive
Bloomington, IN 47403
www.balboapress.com
1 (877) 407-4847

Because of the dynamic nature of the Internet, any web addresses or links contained in this book may have changed since publication and may no longer be valid. The views expressed in this work are solely those of the author and do not necessarily reflect the views of the publisher, and the publisher hereby disclaims any responsibility for them.

The author of this book does not dispense medical advice or prescribe the use of any technique as a form of treatment for physical, emotional, or medical problems without the advice of a physician, either directly or indirectly. The intent of the author is only to offer information of a general nature to help you in your quest for emotional and spiritual well-being. In the event you use any of the information in this book for yourself, which is your constitutional right, the author and the publisher assume no responsibility for your actions.

Any people depicted in stock imagery provided by Thinkstock are models, and such images are being used for illustrative purposes only.
Certain stock imagery © Thinkstock.

Print information available on the last page.

ISBN: 978-1-5043-7895-6 (sc)
ISBN: 978-1-5043-7897-0 (hc)
ISBN: 978-1-5043-7896-3 (e)

Library of Congress Control Number: 2017905875

Balboa Press rev. date: 05/01/2017

Dedication

This book is dedicated to my children, Lily & Ben, who demonstrate every day what it is to be an enlightened being, and to my husband Chris who chose me to be by his side as we walk through life together.

A special thank you and love to my parents and my sister who stood by me as I went on a spiritual journey that was very different from what they knew.

Much gratitude to my friends, Kim and Suzanne

and cousin Stacy for all of your love, help, input and patience!

Thank you Margaret Minardi, for you amazing artistic abilities and beautiful creative design of the book cover.

I am very grateful to my spiritual teachers who have lifted my soul and validated the importance of living an enlightened life. Thank you Esther & Abraham Hicks, Wayne Dyer, Mike Dooley & Joel Osteen.

Introduction

About ten years ago, I developed the gift of mediumship. The ability for me to see, feel and communicate with spirit was thrust upon me after enduring many years of physical challenges and countless number of surgeries. As a matter of fact, throughout these physically challenging years, I often found myself as the client of a spiritual reader asking questions like "Is my health going to be ok?" and "Why is this happening to me?". Although at the time, the responses I heard seemed unrelated and unimpressive, I was often told that "somehow this is all changing you and preparing you to help others". I didn't quite understand what that meant. After many years of frequenting the psychic circuit on a quest for answers to what seemed like the never ending cycle of pain and surgery, I met a reader who stood out from the rest. She came to my home one day to read for me and a group of my friends. It was a gathering, planned on my part, to entertain and distract me from the health challenges I was facing, as at the time I was recovering from yet another surgery. She knew things about me that nobody had told her. She knew personal things about my past and knew that I had a son with special needs. She also took my hands, looked me in the eyes and said, "You are going to be sitting where I am. You too are a medium meant to give messages to others." Although, I have long forgotten exactly who this woman was, I will always remember that moment because that was the day that my life began to change, and as a result, what I am now able to see and feel is forever different.

It was that very same night when it all began for me. Random pictures continuously flashed before me, like looking through a view master. The strange thing was that all of the images seemed to be pointless to me at the time. What did it matter that when I spoke to my girlfriend on the phone, I saw images of the brownies she was baking or the UPS package at her front door? It was all very interesting, but I couldn't comprehend how these fleeting photographs in my mind would help people, or even matter to them at all. It wasn't long after that with these pictures came added information….voices, names, scents, symbols and numbers. This was a whole new language, and if I wanted to learn it, then I needed to study and practice.

At first, I practiced my new found clairvoyance on only my closest of friends. At this point, I was hesitant to disclose to my family what I was experiencing, partly because I wasn't sure how they would react and, partly because I didn't quite understand it myself. I found myself startled when I began to see a pattern developing. When speaking with friends I would often hear a name and then ask my friend what that name meant to them. Too often that response would be that the name is of a close relative, but they are dead! Dead? What? I couldn't wrap my brain around what was really going on here. Was I actually communicating with someone from the other side? Maybe, but I wasn't about to find out. My fear set in, and I called it quits. That is until I received a phone call from my sister early one morning.

Still unaware of my newly found metaphysical experiences, my sister called me one morning to ask me "Are you okay?" When I said "Yes, why?, she replied, "Well, I had the strangest dream about you last night. I dreamt that God came to me and said to tell you to keep doing what it is that you are doing because it is very important and you are protected and loved." I am so grateful to my sister for relaying that message because she didn't realize the significance that it held. That was such a pivotal day for me on this journey because it was at that point that I embraced my gift, let go of the fear, and began my work as a medium. I was called to be a messenger to deliver validations, love and support to people from their loved ones who have crossed over.

Years have now passed and I am so grateful for my experiences working as a medium. I am grateful to have brought healing to others and to be part of the awakening that people experience when they receive messages and validations from loved ones on the other side. I have learned so much through the psychic medium readings, a lot of which has been to my surprise. I have learned that we are all eternal spirit. I have learned that we came into our lives for the love, joy, experiences and growth. I have learned about how God and the Universe are working with us daily to help us manifest all of our desires. I have learned that we have amazing inner guidance which is meant to help us feel our way through our life path. I have learned that when we raise our vibration up closer to God then we have the power to create a truly magical life.

My mission now is to share all that I have learned through my many years of communication with spirit. I am so grateful to now be able to share what I know about energy, spirit and vibration and to teach others about lifting up their vibration so they can lead the life they are meant to and experience the love, joy, health and abundance that God wants for them. Once you become aware of this you will always want to "Enlighten Up".

Where is your dimmer?

Early on in my work as a medium, I learned that there is something called "vibration", or the movement of energy. I also learned that there are many different levels of vibration. It became more and more evident to me that we are energy and spirits are energy and God is energy and in order for me to connect as a medium, I was lifting up my vibration and tuning into the vibration of spirit (almost like tuning into a higher radio station). The more I did this, the easier it became for me to get up there. What I never expected was the level of fatigue that hit me after a few straight hours of reading. Total exhaustion would come over me. However, the more I thought about this, the more it made sense. I was using my energy to lift my vibration and connection to the higher vibration of the spirit world. After readings, I would come crashing down. I couldn't hold myself in this vibration for long. Ironically, this is the pattern we all have as humans in regard to our own vibration. We all have levels of vibration within us. It's as if we all have an internal light dimmer, just like a dimmer in a room. When we raise our dimmer up we are shining bright. We are on a high vibration. We feel good. We are happy. Things are easy and clear. When we lower our dimmer our world becomes darker. We are depressed and anxious. We live from fear.

It took me some time to really get it, but the more I practiced lifting my vibration, the more apparent it was. When we focus on the good things in our lives, our blessings, what we love, what feels good to us, then we raise our dimmer. We lift our vibration and are living from our own spirit, our soul, closest to God. When we focus on what we are afraid of, what we worry about, what we don't want or don't have, then we lower our dimmer and disconnect ourselves from the high vibration of God.

Just like my work as a medium, if you lift yourself too far too quickly, you may come crashing down. The challenge for most is to break the habits of thought they have created and to get into a place of belief in themselves and the world around them. Like training for a marathon, this doesn't happen in a day. But if you get out there and do a little more training each day, create a little more awareness each day, lift your dimmer a little higher each day, then you teach yourself to hold a high vibration for the majority of your days and will create a healthier, happier, easier, more abundant life. You will live the life of joy you came here to experience.

So, the question is "where is your dimmer?" In the following chapters I will be teaching and guiding you on ways to lift your dimmer so you can "enlighten up"!

Enlighten Up:

There are always signs available to you to let you know that God and all of the powers of the Universe are with you. Embrace the signs.

The signs of spirit are always there for you. Signs that God is with you, that the angels are near, that your loved ones crossed over have never really left you, are everywhere for you. The signs are there to comfort you, to bring you peace, to guide you, uplift you and validate what you already know. The question is, is your dimmer up high enough to receive them?

I have heard countless numbers of stories over the years about signs received from loved ones who have crossed over. Many clients, and friends, have shared with me their experience of seeing repetitive numbers, animals, birds, flowers, rainbows, hearing songs and names, smelling perfume, cigarette or cigar smoke etc. I love these stories and can't hear them often enough. I love the peace it brings for people to become aware that there really is more than what the eyes can see.

Spirit is very playful. Your guides, angels and loved ones on the other side love to hear from you. If you have a question, they will answer. They will do what they can from their highest of vibration to send you a sign or symbol to provide the confirmation and reassurance that you are seeking. What I have learned as a medium who intentionally raises her vibration to communicate with spirit, is that the higher your vibration…the brighter your dimmer… the clearer and more obvious these signs and symbols become.

When you receive a sign from spirit it is important to validate back to them that you "get it". For example, if you asked a loved one to send you a flower as a sign that they are with you, and you receive a random rose that day, it's important to acknowledge your awareness and appreciate the communication. The more you do this, the more the communication will continue and become easier and more natural for you.

As I began my work as a medium, I often asked for signs and validations from God that this is what I was meant to do. It was such an unexpected life path change for me, causing me to constantly seek reassurance. It was as if overnight, I received a whole different set of eyes and ears, along with which came a lot of fear, mostly of the unknown and that something "bad" could come to me.

One day, early on in my work as a medium, I sat in meditation asking God to show me a sign that I was protected. It was the day before my son's birthday party. I asked for a sign and then began to get my children ready to go to a party supply store. I brought myself into a state of wonderment of how and when God would answer me. We opened the front door to go out to the car and to my astonishment, there was a tremendous turtle on my front steps just sitting there. I had no idea how he got there or where he came from. He was huge and somehow got himself onto the very top step. I didn't think much of it in the spiritual sense, but I was in shock to see him there. We then went out our back door to get to the car because there was no way around this turtle. When at the party store, I told both my kids that they could each pick out something very small to bring home with them that day. My daughter chose a yo-yo and my son a hand clapper toy. We left the store and when we returned home, we noticed that the turtle was no longer there. I then unloaded my packages and handed my kids the toys they chose. It was at this time that I noticed something that I didn't notice while in the store. Both my daughter's yo-yo and my son's hand clapper had a picture of a turtle on it. I knew better than to believe this was a coincidence. I learned very early on while communicating with spirits that there truly are no coincidences. It hit me right at that moment. God was trying to get a message to me. When I saw the giant turtle on my steps, I didn't recognize it as a sign or message, but now seeing pictures of two more turtles woke me up. This is what I call "synchronicity". God, spirits and the angels talk to you through signs and symbols. When you miss it the first time, they will show it to you again and again in a different way, hoping that you will notice. Luckily, my dimmer was up and I noticed. Then, I ran to my computer and googled the spiritual significance of a turtle. It was a direct answer to my request to God to please show me a sign I was protected. A turtle represents protection, as it can retreat under its hard shell at any time for safety. WOW! It doesn't get clearer than that. There was nothing to fear. I was like the turtle with protection all around me.

A client of mine, shared with me her personal story of asking to receive a sign from her brother who had passed away suddenly. Very soon after the news that her brother had died, she began talking to him and asked him for a sign that he was safe. The next day, as she walked her dogs on a hiking trail, she noticed something shiny on the ground. She picked it up and saw that it was a silver heart pin. This trail was the last place she had seen her brother. As she placed the pin in her bag, she wondered if this could be his sign to her. The following day, she took her daughter shopping to buy a dress for the funeral. She noticed a shiny object in the dressing room. As she reached for it, she realized it was a glittery silver heart pin. She realized the synchronicity here, yet still asked for more. She thought to herself, three times the charm, as she asked for this heart symbol to continue to be shown to her. In the mail, the next day, she received a sympathy card. Inside the card was an angel pin. It was silver and shaped like a heart. She went on to receive more silver heart pins as the days went on. In total she received five silver heart pins in the five days following his passing. When spirit knows you are asking for a sign, they give it to you. When you acknowledge the sign and ask for more, they give it to you. All you need to do is look for it with hope and expectancy.

Expectation is a key factor in receiving signs from the spirit realm. If you don't really believe, if you come from a place of fear or doubt then it lowers your internal dimmer and separates you from the vibration of God, your guides, the angels and your loved ones on the other side, where your signs already are. Expect to be guided. Expect to see, feel or hear a sign. Not only is this comforting, but it creates magic in your day!

Enlighten Up:

Stop saying that life is HARD and start saying that life is EASY!

I have noticed all too frequently when listening to my clients that they feel life is hard for them, and sadly, most of them believe that it's supposed to be that way. But the truth is, it's not. Life is meant to be fun and things are meant to be much easier than we create them to be. We create them to be difficult by affirming over and over to ourselves that it's too difficult. Not only do we affirm it, but we hear it throughout the day from others as well. When we hear and think something over and over again, it becomes a belief and when we believe something to be a certain way, it will be that way. Therefore, we have allowed ourselves to fall into the trap of believing and creating things to be much harder than they really are.

Become aware and take notice of how often you hear yourself saying "it's hard" or "it's difficult".

When you catch yourself in the midst of that affirmation, stop and laugh and think to yourself, "Wow I really have created a habit of thinking that this (particular subject) is hard in my life." Then repeat to yourself "this may be easier than I believe it to be" and "things are getting a little easier each day." Also, pay attention to how often you hear others around you affirming that their life, or a part of it, is hard or challenging. You will then begin to create an awareness for yourself that many others hold this belief, which has only been making it more challenging for you to believe differently. The goal here is to create an awareness that how we think it to be....it becomes. So, if we think it will be hard (paying the bills, finding a relationship, finding a good job, feeling well, etc.) and continue to think it will be hard, then we have created a belief that life is hard and so it will become.

BUT....you are a powerful, spiritual being and there is great power in your mind and your thoughts. If you can start to shift towards the thought that the parts of your life that now feel difficult may become easier and easier, then it will.

Try saying these "Enlighten Up" affirmations daily to help you raise your dimmer and create an easier life:

"Life is so EASY"

"Things that I desire flow EASILY to me"

"I will get through this with EASE"

"Things are getting a little EASIER each day"

Enlighten Up:

Stop asking others what they think you should do because the answers are within YOU!

Many people have come to me for a reading to connect to their loved ones crossed over. However, others have come to get my "psychic" impression about a question they have regarding their life path. The truth is, the answer to these questions are not in the cards, they are inside of you.

How often do you seek the opinions of others? It is so common for us when we are feeling confused or trying to make a decision to ask everyone around us what they would do. We ask and we ask, hoping someone else will be able to bring us clarity. Have you noticed that asking others for advice or their opinion of your circumstances often brings you more confusion?

People come from different energy vibrations and different perspectives. Everyone has their own unique set of lenses to the world around them. When you ask others for help solving your problems, they are looking at things from where THEIR energy stands, which can be very different from where YOUR energy stands. That is why we often do not resonate with the advice others give us. You have the ability to go deep within yourself, where all of the answers for you are.

As you continue on your journey, observe how often you ask others for their opinion. If you are seeking clarity or trying to make a decision, sit quietly with yourself and ask yourself how it FEELS to YOU. Your feelings are your best guide. You are looking for what FEELS better inside of YOU and that is what brings you to clarity. What feels good to you is not necessarily what would feel good to another, which is why going deep within yourself is where your best guidance comes from.

When you learn to go within for guidance and answer your own questions and decisions based on your own feelings and emotions, you can never go wrong. The more you practice, the easier it becomes!

Enlighten Up:

Stop looking at all that you don't have yet, and start looking at all that you do have now!

In my practice, I have frequently seen the pattern of people focused on what they do not have. Clients have easily become emotional regarding the fact that they do not have something they have been wanting for a very long time. Commonly, people become upset over having trouble finding their ideal job or meeting a significant other. Others feel they are lacking money to pay their bills, take a vacation, or make a particular purchase they have long desired. In general, we tend to look at the lack in our life, things we don't have yet but want. We become frustrated that we don't see certain things in our lives that we see in the lives of others. We wonder why certain things came to others so easily that we struggle to receive. We begin to focus more on what is not there instead of what is. But what we don't realize is that this type of focus actually blocks us from receiving what we want.

Trust me, God and the Universe know exactly what it is that you desire. But it's much more difficult for you to receive it from a place of worry, fear or doubt. These low vibration feelings lower your dimmer and disconnect you from the vibration of God, where all the things you want flow easily to you. When we live from a place of constantly noticing what we don't have, we are not allowing ourselves to receive what is already there for us. When we choose to live from a place of gratitude for all of our blessings and all that we do have right now, then all the things that we want come to us faster. The positive focus raises your dimmer and when your vibration is up it's as if magic happens.

From this moment on, do your best to be happy

now, without whatever it is that you want to receive. If you find yourself talking to others about what you don't have then take a few moments afterwards, look at your life, look at your home, your friends, your family, all of your blessings and start to notice all of the little things that you do have that are right in front of you right now. Write them down if you can, or simply take a few moments to feel the fullness of them.

I am so grateful to have learned this in my own life. I was also in the habit of focusing on what I was lacking for a very long time. As I learned more about energy, the Universe and vibration through my work, I began to pay closer attention to my words and my focus. I would often affirm lack of money by using phrases like "I don't have the money for that" or "I can't afford it" etc. I consciously and intentionally started to change that. For a long time I had wanted this very large angel statue for my office. I would admire it often in this particular store, and it was pricy. I realized that when I would see it, I would feel sad and think to myself that I wish I could buy it, if only I had the money. After becoming more and more aware of how I was focusing my thoughts, I entered the same store one day. There was that beautiful angel statue right up front. I walked over to it to admire it. I gave it love and positive focus, as I noticed even more details of how beautiful it was. The sales clerk approached me, as I must have been standing in front of it for ten straight minutes. She asked me if I wanted to purchase it. I said, "Yes, I do". But this time, my response was very different. I told the saleswoman that I will be back to purchase it very soon and I am so excited for the day when I bring it home with me. I then left the store, empty handed, but happy and hopeful. I really began to believe that I will have the statue one day and I allowed myself to feel the joy of that. Then, I let it go. Three days later, I received a text from a friend (who knew nothing about the angel I wanted). She asked me to meet her outside my home because she was dropping off a gift for me to thank me for helping her through a difficult time. I had no expectation of what it could be….but, you guessed it…..it was my beautiful angel statue! It was brought to me by the Universe because my focus had shifted onto the feeling of excitement and hope instead of lack. I had raised my dimmer when thinking about this angel and then it simply just came. That's how the Universe works. God can bring anything to you easily and effortlessly when you can bring yourself into joyful anticipation of it, when you raise your dimmer up!

There are many things in our lives that we have once wanted that we now do have. Spend some time reflecting on this. Look for things that you have once desired that wasn't in your life that you now have and can see. I bet you can name so many things. Write them down. As you talk about things that you have manifested and created into your life by lifting up your dimmer, as you give that attention and gratitude, then you are speeding up receiving more from God. It really is that simple.

Enlighten Up:

Let go of "how" things will happen and trust that the dots are always being connected by God and the Universe.

I believe that one of the most challenging parts of getting one's energy and vibration up is that people tend to get stuck in worrying about HOW something will happen. Worrying about the how and asking questions like "how will this ever happen?" will definitely lower your dimmer. Also, many times we put limits on the "how" in our minds. For example, many of my clients have shared the same limiting thought about how they will receive more money. Some have shared with me that the only way they expect to receive more money is by working overtime, getting a second job or winning the lottery. Others have limiting beliefs as to how they will meet a significant other, assuming it will only come from online dating or being set up by someone.

The point here is that when we try to figure out how God is going to bring to us what we are asking for, then we actually limit the unlimited ways it can be done. The Universe is vast and there is unlimited abundance for everyone. Just because one person has something or one million people have the same thing, doesn't mean that there isn't enough for you too. When we ask the Universe for something, such as money, and we limit our expectation of the means of which we can receive it, then we are blocking out countless other possible ways it can be brought to us.

Simply put, the how is not your job to figure out. Your job is simple, to ask for what you want and then to keep your dimmer up through hope and faith that it will be brought to you. God and the powers of the Universe will then line it up for you in ways that you would never expect. Letting go of how can be scary, but it's also quite amazing because you then realize you can receive things in ways that you would have never, ever expected.

When I learned to let go of how things can come about, I realized even more how much power there is in keeping our energy positive and trusting that when we ask for something, it is always given (just not always in ways that we expect it to be given). This became incredibly evident to me through an amazing story of how my son received a very special therapy dog. My son, Ben, is on the autism spectrum. Years ago, when he was about 3 years old, we became very concerned about the fact that he would wander along our property. We decided to try to get him a therapy dog not only for companionship, but for his safety as well. I researched different means of receiving a dog for him. At the time, there weren't many options and the wait list could take a few years. Despite these obstacles, we signed up with a foundation. We were required to fundraise thousands of dollars and were told it would be about a year or so to get a puppy, who then stays with a volunteer family while the puppy is in training. The puppy would be brought to our home to pair with our son and have visitations until fully trained, at which time he would transition to live with us. The whole process could take anywhere from one to two years. My husband and I both really wanted this dog for our son much sooner than that. We knew what we wanted, and I knew how the Universe works, and so I began to use my power of lifting my energy through positive thoughts and words and simply brought myself, as well as my family, into a place of excited anticipation for receiving this dog.

I began to strongly practice faith that God can

move things faster when you believe things are working out for you and when you let go of how it will happen. I shared with my children, my family and friends how excited I was for my son to be getting a therapy dog. When asked how long it will take, I explained that the foundation said a year or two, but I am trusting it will move faster than that. We began our fundraising efforts and money started to flow in. Each day my kids and I would play the game of guessing what the dog would look like, what name it would have etc. We even went so far as to make a trip to the pet store to buy bowls for the dog. We acted as if we had to get ready because the dog may come sooner than expected. It was January and I took out our new calendar and circled dates that I would hope to have the dog by. I circled a date in April, knowing very well that was only four months away.

A few weeks later, I went to the food store with my children. Walking around the perimeter of the shopping center was a woman training a guide dog. I have seen guide dog trainers in our town before, but never had the opportunity to stop and talk to one or interact with the dog. As the woman and her dog came closer, we began to have conversation. She was so warm and welcoming and allowed Ben to interact with the dog. I eagerly told her that we too are getting a therapy dog soon. I explained to her that Ben had autism and we were in the process of fundraising for a dog for him through a particular foundation. She knew of that foundation and was very excited for him and wished us luck as she moved on with her training. About an hour later, while driving out of the shopping center, the woman and I crossed paths again. I knew that this was some type of synchronicity from the Universe. She was crossing my path again because I missed something God had wanted me to learn from her the first time we spoke. I pulled my car over and she walked towards the car. She asked me if I live in town and told me she lives nearby as well. She then gave me her phone number and mentioned that after Ben receives his dog, if I ever need any help, I can give her a call because she lives so close to us. She was very kind hearted and sincere. As I thanked her and pulled away, I wondered what the Universe was up to.

About a month went by and my family continued with fundraising efforts and positive talk about receiving a dog. At this point, we had about half of the money we needed. I continued to talk to God and my angels, asking them to speed up the process for us, so my son could have a canine friend and we could have some comfort knowing there was an extra safety measure for him. Soon after, I had a dream that changed everything.

I went to bed one night, talking to my husband about the dog. We were brainstorming another way to raise more funds. To my complete and utter shock, that same night, in my dream, I was told what to do next. I don't know how to describe it except to say that I heard a loud….very loud…male voice speaking to me. The voice was very direct and very insistent. He told me that we needed to change the direction we were taking for getting a dog for Ben. He told me that having a puppy, who makes visits and goes back and forth to live with another family until fully trained, would really upset our son because once he had the dog, he wouldn't be able to let go. He also told me that Ben needed an older dog. I remember getting upset while speaking back to this voice. I told the male voice that I was now very confused, I didn't know what to do next. We had already raised half the money and given it over to the foundation and I wouldn't even know who to call. I was upset and overwhelmed. Then a picture flashed of the woman I met with the guide dog the month before! The voice told me to "call her, she will help you".

I immediately woke my husband in a state of panic. I didn't even know how to explain to him what happened. I wasn't even sure whose voice that was. Was it God? A spirit guide? An angel? I had no idea, but despite how confused I was, I knew that I had to listen to it. I trusted it was meant to guide us towards what was best for Ben. To be honest, a month had passed since I saw the woman at the shopping center and I couldn't even remember her name. I had also changed phones that month and wasn't even sure I still had her number and even if I did, what the heck would I say to her? It was the middle of night and I ran to my cell phone. I couldn't remember her name! I scrolled through my list of contacts and sure enough there it was under "therapy dog". I was apprehensive, but knew I had to call her first thing in the morning.

The next morning, as soon as the time allowed, I made the call. All I could think is that this woman is going to believe I am insane. But quite the opposite happened. She answered the phone and I said "Hello, I doubt you remember me, but I am the woman you met about a month ago at the shopping center. I was the one with a child with autism." She responded immediately, "Of course I remember you, I haven't stopped thinking of your son since we met."

I anxiously proceeded to tell her about my dream. She was so open and receptive and confided in me that she always wanted to somehow help children with special needs receive therapy dogs. She went on to explain to me that the foundation she works for has dogs that get released from their program, which is for the blind. Not all of the dogs that are trained pass the tests for working with the blind, but these dogs can still make an amazing therapy dog because they have been through significant training. We spoke for a while. There was an instant connection between our energies. We ended the conversation with her saying "Let me see what I can do for you." About a month later….in the month of March…. we received a 2 year old lab for our son through her connections. He came with the name "Lucca", meaning light (which I am more than sure was not a coincidence). It is now seven years later and Lucca remains a best friend for our son and security for our family. In addition, the money we had raised for the initial puppy was able to be gifted to another child on their list, who was also trying to raise more funds to receive a dog. We not only were able to receive such a blessing, but also were able to give a blessing to another as well.

Sharing this story is meant to demonstrate to you that when you have the faith that what you ask God for you will receive, when you act as if it's on the way to you, when you let go of how it will come in, then mountains are moved, dots are connected and people and places are lined up to you that you never would have expected. From this point on, when you ask for something that you want, let go of the how, act as if it's on the way to you and enjoy watching how it all unfolds.

Enlighten Up:

From your most challenging days, can come your greatest ideas and inspirations, if you allow it.

I have had the honor of meeting a lot of wonderful people through my readings. Many have come to see me after losing a loved one. After meeting with thousands of clients to help them connect to family crossed over, I have recognized that there are two different ways people tend to grieve. There are people who have lost loved ones and even several years later, have not been able to find any light in their darkness, and there are those who have found the spark in the dark by becoming inspired to do something new or different, to make a positive change. For example, through the experience of loss, some of my clients have created scholarships or foundations in honor of their loved ones, others have written books, poems or songs, some have advocated for a change in a law and others have traveled to places they know their family member always wanted to go, in order to feel a deeper connection. Whatever the inspired thought or choice may be, when you can move towards it during your dark time, and give it some of your positive focus and attention, then you can slowly raise your dimmer back up and begin to feel some joy again.

There is no denying that challenges, such as losing a loved one, can bring us to a dark place of sadness and depression. Grief, despair and depression are some of the lowest of vibrations. When we are in those feelings, it is typically because something happened to us that we really didn't want to happen. However, it's truly up to us as to how long we will allow our dimmers to stay on their lowest level. It's natural to have a really low dimmer sometimes, but, when you stay there too long, it's as if you shut off the internal light of your spirit. No matter what is happening in your life, be it the loss of a loved one, loss of a job, health issues or money trouble, your inner spirit still wants to shine. Your soul is meant to glow. It wants to live and experience happiness for as long as you have your physical life.

There will always be obstacles and hurdles in life. A physical existence is filled with so many of them. However, if you allow it, these difficult times can teach you what you want and create inspiration inside of you. So, as you move forward in your life and are faced with your next challenge, ask yourself if you can find the light within the darkness. Look for the new path it brings you. Observe the new people, places and things that come your way because of it. This will help you to enlighten up!

Enlighten Up:

You are always in the right place at the right time. You have the incredible advantage of perfect timing from the Universe.

Have you ever turned left when you meant to turn right? That's because the Universe is always guiding and helping us to change our course of direction in order to bring us to the right place at the right time. God connects the dots to bring us what we are asking for with divine timing. Until I began to understand and trust this timing, I would become frustrated and annoyed if something happened in my day such as misplacing my keys or leaving something at home and having to turn around to go back. However, I have heard from so many people in my readings as to how they can look back at something that at the time seemed quite inconvenient and now recognize that the timing was actually a set up for them to receive what they were asking for.

A special story of spirit visiting a friend in a dream has become my favorite example of the intricate and intentional timing of the Universe. About six years ago, a young man, Eddie, visited me for a reading. One of his closest friends, who was only a teenager at the time, had died in a sudden accident not long before. As I began to read Eddie, this young male energy came through with messages. He spoke about a trip Eddie was soon taking to Mexico with his family. He said that there would be a lot of gate changes at the airport and to trust the timing of that. Shortly after his return from his trip, Eddie came in to see me again. He shared with me this incredible story of spirit and timing.

A few days before the trip, Eddie had a visitation in his dream from his friend. This is a common way that spirit connects to their loved ones. Because sleep allows us to be in a more relaxed state, our vibration is up and spirits can more easily connect to us. Eddie began to describe his experience to me. He told me that he was "sucked out" of his dream and that everything was black and white expect for his friend, who appeared in color. He said that the friend then brought him to the scene of his accident. He showed Eddie pictures of his family and thanked him for all of the candles that had been lit for him. Eddie started saying things like "this can't be real", "you're not real" etc. His friend then replied, "Yes, this is real and you will see me between 9 and 10." Also, while in this dream state, Eddie noticed that he had a cell phone on him. At this point, a text came to that phone which read, "Look for me between 9 and 10".

After the visitation happened, Eddie could not connect any significance to the numbers 9 and 10. A few days later, he arrived at the airport for his trip. The first thing that became apparent was the gate number for his flight kept changing, which was a validation from his reading. The gate change happened three times, until eventually it was confirmed that their flight was boarding at gate 11. As Eddie neared the gate, he realized he had to use the bathroom. He told the others to go ahead of him and he would meet them at gate 11. When Eddie came out of the bathroom and was walking towards gate 11, he recognized a group of people waiting to board a plane near another gate. He recognized them because they were all wearing shirts that were made in honor of Eddie's friend! Soon after Eddie's friend crossed over, a foundation was made in his name, by his family. The shirts had his friend's name on it. In fact, Eddie had the same shirt in the same color, so it was very easy for him to notice this. They stopped for a quick moment to talk about where they were headed. It was at this moment that Eddie realized he was standing between gates 9 and 10! Everything clicked in that moment with his dream. He saw an incredible sign from his friend, just as he said he would, between 9 and 10!

When your dimmer is up, you respond to the gentle nudges from the Universe. It's as if you are working in sync, together. God is sending you impulses and you are receiving them. In this story, Eddie received the impulse to go to the bathroom. If he hadn't been a few minutes behind his family, then he would not have seen the group of people wearing shirts with his friend's name on it, between gates 9 and 10. Minutes or even seconds of changing your direction is bringing you to exactly where you are supposed to be. So, the next time you lose your keys or can't find your other shoe as you are trying to rush out the door, try not to feel inconvenienced. Instead, recognize it as your perfect timing.

Enlighten Up:

The best gift you can give to someone is your own happiness.

Many people I have read over the years have referred family and friends to come in as well. While some of these referrals come in with their own belief in the process of connecting to spirit, others have come in because they felt pressured to receive a reading. It is amazing how different the experience is when the person being read really does not want to be there. People have good intentions when recommending my services to a friend or family member, however if the vibration of someone is very low and their belief in the afterlife is non-existent, then they don't always receive the messages that are being delivered. It's sort of like they hear what I am saying, but don't resonate with it or really connect to it. Like anything else in life, when we believe, then we receive.

Often people are hoping they can bring someone happiness or peace, or help someone shift out of depression by leading them to the same person, place or thing that they found to be helpful. Some people purchase gift certificates for healing services for others, or buy them a self-help book that they have read. I'm not saying that this never works, what I am saying is that if the person on the receiving end is not on an energy vibration of allowing their energy to shift, it can't work.

It is very difficult to watch people we care about become sad, worried, depressed or anxious. We often want to fix their problems so they can be happy and we can enjoy a relationship with them again. We purchase gifts, cards and flowers to try to cheer people up. We just want to see others with their dimmers up because we know that's who they really are and we naturally want to connect to the loving, joyful spirit inside the person. However, it is not our job to raise someone's dimmer. Actually, we are not able to raise the dimmer of another person and when we keep looking at other's problems and focus on their negative emotions, then we are lowering our own dimmer to do so. People have to raise their own vibration. It takes the realization that you are living with your internal light out and desire to reconnect to your inner being. We all have the ability to shift ourselves and find our own happiness. It simply takes desire to do so and belief that it's possible. When you have the desire and the belief, then God will line up the people, places and things for you to help you find your true self again.

As you continue on your journey, you will of course encounter a friend or loved one who has moments, days, weeks or years of low vibration emotions. Know that the best thing you can do for them is continue to be happy. Don't look too long at their problems or try to pull them up when they are resistant. Simply lead by your own happiness. Teach by example that there is joy to be had in this life. As you continue to allow yourself to shine around them, chances are that over time, they will want to enlighten up so they can join you.

Enlighten Up:

Listen more to the children around you. They often speak from their soul.

Since my spiritual work began, I have had the pleasure of working with many children. I actually prefer working with children because their vibrations are so high. They haven't yet settled completely into the negativity of society around them. They are eager to feel happy because they are still very connected to their inner being. Many children are very interested in talking about spiritual topics such as God, dreams and angels. More than anything, I love sitting with kids and having these discussions. If I listen carefully enough, I often learn a thing or two.

Before working as a medium, I never gave much thought to past lives. Although growing up I had many questions about different religions, I never really questioned if I had a past life or if living many different lifetimes is a possibility. However, once I began working with children, it became evident to me that we live many lifetimes. Over the years, children have shared with me not only memories of being somebody else, but memories of how they have died in past lives. I have also heard from parents, amazing stories of their child's past life recall. One mother once shared with me a story of her driving over a bridge heading to Manhattan, when her young child pointed out the window to the river and said "Mommy, that's where I died one time." More clearly than adults, children still hold these memories. They are not as grounded as we are. They don't live as much from the ego as we do. They live from the soul and many still have memory of what it was like before entering this physical life.

Children holding onto to memories from their time as a spirit became very apparent to me through conversation with my daughter, Lily. It was very difficult for me to conceive Lily. I tried for five years to get pregnant and was told by fertility doctors that I had a two percent chance of ever conceiving. After many disappointments with failed IVF attempts, my husband and I started adoption procedures. Sadly, at the same time we were working towards adoption, my grandfather developed cancer and was put on hospice. My husband and I would visit him frequently. Even in his weakened state, each time he saw me, he would ask me if I was pregnant yet. Time after time, I would tell him that I am adopting a baby. He seemed comforted by my reply. One afternoon, towards his very last days, I went to see him and stood by his bedside. He was obviously sedated on pain medicine. I held his hand and said, "Hi grandpa, it's me." He opened his eyes and looked at me, smiled and said, "I see your baby girl". In this moment, I believed my grandfather was delusional and it was the drugs that were talking. My grandfather passed away one week later in August 2002. I received the incredible news that I was pregnant in January 2003. Lily was born nine months later.

Seven years later, when Lily was a second grader, something very unusual happened. I received a call one afternoon from the school psychologist at Lily's elementary school. He began the conversation by expressing his sympathy for the loss of my grandfather. He was assuming it was recent. He followed this by telling me that Lily spent an hour in his office that day because she was crying over the death of her great grandfather. He said he comforted her for a while and she was then able to return to class. I was so taken back by this phone call and felt uncomfortable to explain to this nice man that Lily never met her great grandfather because he died before she was born. I wondered what was really happening here. I simply thanked him for his time spent with Lily and for his concern and reassured him that I will speak with her more about this when she gets home. When Lily got off the bus that afternoon, I could tell by her eyes that she had been crying. After she settled in, I asked her about her day. She told me that her teacher sent her down to the school psychologist because she had been crying in class. When I asked her why she was crying, she said because she misses Pop Pop, my grandfather. Completely confused by this I told Lily that I know it's very sad when someone that we love dies, but that I didn't understand why she would randomly cry over Pop Pop, being that he died so long ago, and she never knew him. It was at this point that I realized there was a much bigger picture here. Lily looked at me, exhausted, and somewhat angrily, she replied, "I am so tired of people thinking I didn't know Pop Pop. I knew him when I was in heaven and he was there too. I spent time with him there and now I miss him. Somedays I just want to see him again." WOW! I had no words really, just a moment of total awe and belief that her soul somehow knew my grandfather's soul, and somehow she still remembers that. Honestly, I hope she never forgets, because I know I won't.

Even when Lily was a toddler, I could tell that she was very connected to spirit. At the age of two, she had many "imaginary" friends that I knew were not imaginary. She was very specific as to what they looked like and would describe their physical traits in detail to me. As she became a preschooler, she began to describe what she would call her "angel" to me. She was a woman with dark hair and jewels on her dress that had beads around the waistline. One day when she was six years old and had a playdate of a few friends over, she confided in me afterward that her angel watched over all of her friends that day as they played, but left the room when they ate pizza. She would speak very matter of fact about her angel, as if it were typical for every child to have one. After meeting with many children and families over the years now, I know that this is not so out of the ordinary. Having imaginary friends seems to be a common occurrence amongst toddlers. Also, parents have shared numerous stories with me about their toddlers pointing to what seems like nothing in a room, while saying the name of their grandparent or family member who has crossed over, as if they are acutally seeing them.

As children get older, they tend to lose their sensitivity to the spirits around them, as well as their memories of them. They become more integrated in a society that has learned to disconnect from their higher selves and lower their dimmers. Their spiritual gifts often get dismissed as being their imagination and they learn to ignore this connection and live a life more from the ego. As you move on in your days, take more time to observe children and listen to their words. Engage in conversation with them about their thoughts on God and the angels. Ask them detailed questions about their dreams. Encourage them to keep their dimmers up and their connection to their inner being strong. Don't let your own fears or low energy dim a child's inner light. Children don't only learn from their parents and teachers, but they are teaching us as well. Challenge yourself to listen to them. They are here to remind us that life is meant to be fun and playful, and that we all have an inner spirit that wants to shine. Children truly know what it means to "enlighten up".

Enlighten Up:

Don't take for granted the miracles that surround you all day.….the sun, moon, trees, children, animals, oceans, stars. Enjoy them all!

Most people wake up and begin their day thinking about their "to do" list. They are living a lifestyle of hurry, rush and go as they try to fit everything into their day. Many of my clients have a common complaint of feeling overwhelmed and struggling to find balance. They are going through the day missing the beauty and miracles that surround them because they are stressed out and their energy is drained. They Universe is presenting miracles to us all day, every day, to keep us uplifted. But when our dimmer is low, we take them for granted as we simply pass them by.

Society as a whole is not helpful or conducive to us realizing all the beauty and miracles that surround us. We tend to wake up to news broadcasts and social media highlighting depressing and fear based stories of what's happening in our world. It would be much more to our benefit if we woke up listening to stories emphasizing the beauty in the world, the kindness in peoples' hearts, the support we have for one another and the unlimited possibilities of the day. It's so important to start your day off on the highest vibration that you can. This sets the tone for your day. If listening to the news or reading something on social media doesn't feel good to you, if it doesn't put joy in your heart, then it's not serving you well. Start your day by tuning into what feels good for you. Whether it's listening to music, reading the comics or going for a walk outside, do what you can to start your day with your vibe up!

Just as important as it is to begin your day with your dimmer up, it's just as important to take time out of your day to keep it up. Up until recently, I was living my life rushing through my days, always feeling that if I stopped, I was being unproductive. However, after years of learning about energy, I realized that when I do stop, and take time out to simply be, then I am more productive and things flow much more easily afterwards. Taking time out of your day to sit quietly for a few minutes, meditate, or give gratitude to what is around you is a great way to quiet the chatter in your mind and raise your dimmer.

Most people are rushing through the day just to get to tomorrow. It is so important to be in the present. When you are able to make the shift to live in the now, your life will only change for the better. There are so many little things around you to appreciate that you will notice more when you slow down. Allow yourself to take the time to give gratitude to your surroundings and all the blessings throughout the day. As you go to bed at night, reflect on the day and name the things that you really loved most about it. This allows you to fall asleep with a good vibe, which will create a more relaxed and peaceful dream state.

Enlighten Up:

Be kind to others, even if they're not kind to you. I bet if you knew their story, you would want to give them a hug.

As a result of reading as a medium for thousands of people over the years, I have learned that everyone has a story, and many of them are heart wrenching. I have read for people who have lost children suddenly and tragically, for parents whose children have unsolved murders, for family members of those who have committed suicide, for countless people who have lost a spouse or parent be it from car accidents, cancers, or other illnesses. I have looked one too many times into the eyes of mothers and fathers who are trying to find a way to move on after the loss of a baby. There are families from years ago that I will never forget because of the shocking story they have experienced. Because of my empathic nature and ability to feel what others are feeling, this has been the most difficult part of this spiritual work for me. I would often cry during a reading and continue to cry after the person has left. Many times because of this, I would need to stop reading altogether, it was too sad for me. But somehow I always found my way back because I know my work is not only to connect messages from loved ones crossed over, but even more importantly, to help people find the light in the their darkness.

We all hear tragic stories around us in society and we often think thank God that's not happening to me. But the truth is, that these low vibration stories have happened to many people around you. Many of those that you interact with in your day, whether it's the gas attendant pumping your gas, your child's teacher, the receptionist at the doctor's office, the telemarketer calling your home, the mailman or the person standing next to you online at the store, have a story of their own that would surprise you. Most of them are doing their best to work past their own feelings of loss, sadness and insecurities.

While moving past a tough divorce, a client of mine named Christina was thrilled to meet a man named Michael. He seemed to be everything she was in search of. He was kind hearted, giving, compassionate and loyal. They had an instant connection. However, she quickly became frustrated with this other side of Michael. At times, he would become cold, inconsiderate and distant. They were in a frequent cycle of breaking up and getting back together. At times, she would share with me things he would do or say that caused her to truly believe he wasn't really the one for her after all. It would be so easy to listen to these stories and pass judgment on Michael, to scrutinize him and infer that he simply is not a nice guy. But, Michael, like many other people, has a story.

When only four years old, Michael's dad passed away from metastatic cancer after being given only six months to live. Michael's dad had been an attorney. He grew up in an upper class home with comfortable surroundings. Surprisingly, his father left no life insurance for Michael's family and they quickly went from living abundantly, to living in a rent controlled apartment with social assistance. Subsequently, Michael's mom had a breakdown and became an alcoholic. For the most part, he learned to take care of himself. He has memories as a 10 year old boy pushing shopping carts for people at the grocery store, in hopes of receiving quarters so he could buy himself food. He also has memories of throwing a school desk out a window, after a teacher asked him if his father would be attending parent teacher conference. He grew up holding onto this pain, with his dimmer down. What Christina was experiencing was dating a man who was trying to bring his dimmer up, so he could live from his soul and enjoy a loving relationship, but was struggling with painful memories of his past which he was allowing to lower his dimmer back down. I am so thrilled to say that Michael has since learned to shift his focus more towards where he is going then where he has been. He started to live more in the now and for his future than allow his energy to get weighed down by his past pains and sorrows. As he lifted his vibration up more and more, his story began to change to the one he has always wanted and Michael and Christina are soon to be married.

Unfortunately, not everyone is able to easily

adjust their light dimmers because they have been in the dark for too long and they become comfortable there. Even though it may not be the life some people desire, they often stay on a low vibe because it's become a habit for them for so many years to live focused on their story of pain and suffering. You do not have to join them there. You should never sacrifice your own happiness. Your number one job should always be to keep your inner light shining. However, as you move through your days and become frustrated by the attitude or curtness that someone may have toward you, remind yourself that you don't know their story. Chances are they are stuck on a low vibration because they are not yet able to raise their dimmer. They are still reacting to something tragic or depressing from their own lives. Be kind even if another is unkind. Be grateful even if another seems ungrateful. Be compassionate even when another is uncompassionate. This may not be easy for you at first, but the more you do it, the better your own vibration will become, which results in having more tolerance and patience for those whose dimmers aren't as bright as yours. Remember, their actions or words towards you has nothing to do with you, but your reaction towards them has everything to do with you.

Enlighten Up:

God, the angels, and your loved ones on the other side are so enamored with you. They couldn't love you more.

The number one question I have been asked by those I have read for over the years has been if their loved one on the other side is happy. The answer to this is YES! I have been very blessed with the ability to feel, see and know spirit energy. When I connect to the energy of loved ones crossed over, or to angels, or God, it all is simply pure positive energy. God is the highest vibration of energy, pure love. As soon as our loved ones cross over, they return to the same vibration. They go back to being pure love as well, where all that exists are high vibration feelings.

Over the years, I have had the honor of experiencing, on a few occasions, very strong visitations with angels and family members of my own who have crossed over. One day, a few years ago, something happened in my personal life that caused me to respond with great fear. I quickly started praying to Archangel Michael, the angel of protection. In seconds, the entire room filled with the brightest of white lights I could ever imagine. I wasn't able to see anything else in the room, as if I was blinded by the light. I felt my body wrapped in heat, like a tremendous warm hug. It was the most comforting, peaceful feeling that immediately removed all fear from my mind. The feeling of love emanating from these angels and spirits is like a love you have never felt before. The amount of love you have for your children, parents or spouse, take that love and multiply it by a million, that's what this feels like. This connection isn't just there for me, it's there for all of us. You just have to ask the angels and God to surround you and believe that they are there for you. That's what allows you to receive.

We are all living here on Earth, in a physical body,

having a physical life experience. It's hard for many to wrap their brains around such things as spirit, angels, God, energy, vibration, eternal life etc. That's because when we are thinking about it, we are often using our minds, or brain, which is very ego based and not using our own spirit or soul to remember who we really are. To live your best, happiest, most peaceful life, it is so important to find who you really are. It's important to connect to your own spirit, the part of you that is all love, non-judgmental and filled with faith. It's there inside of you, sometimes we are simply disconnected to it. Try wearing a different set of lenses to the Universe around you, try seeing and feeling what you can't see with your with your eyes or feel with your hands. Ask for this connection. Ask God to help you. When you ask, it is always given.

Your loved ones on the other side are eternally

happy. They simply cannot feel any other way. They are not angry with you, judging you or critical of your actions here. They checked their egos at the door as soon as they returned to being a soul. They continue to be focused on you and all that you do from where they are. They love you unconditionally and are not holding onto any hurt, pain, or unfinished business. They want for you to find your joy, to let go of sadness and to live your life to the fullest while you are here. Each life experience is temporary, but the soul is eternal. They want you to trust in the eternal connection. They want you to raise your dimmer so they can communicate with you. They are waiting for you to "enlighten up".

Printed in the United States
By Bookmasters